Table of Contents

Lessons

How to Get
WHAT YOU WANT
AND MAKE
Your Parents
PROUD TOO

Publisher: Relationship Counseling Tools, LLC

1st Edition

ISBN: 978-1-7369216-4-7

How to Get What You Want and Make Your Parents Proud Too

My name is Jonah Matthews and at the time of writing this book I am twelve years old. The purpose of this book is to help those around my age learn ways to be their best self as a kid for their parents and peers. I'm inspired by the passion my dad has to help others as a marriage and family therapist. When I found out he was writing a book, I was motivated to write my own as well. So I started thinking, how can I help kids around my age? I realized every kid needs to ask for things. So I compiled twenty-two real-life stories of my experiences, with three key traits I feel you need to make your parents proud (and get what you want!). I hope you enjoy it.

Jonah Matthews

Heated Battle

I was upstairs in my room playing a video game online with my friend John, when I heard my mom yell from downstairs that it was time to come down and eat lunch. Instead of pausing the game I chose to continue to play and ignore my mom's request.

We were in a back-and-forth battle and the match was intense. I am very competitive and that leads to me locking in on whatever I am doing, because I like to win. A few minutes later my mom came up the stairs and cut the game off. I was very upset because I had the lead and the game could not be saved.

Later that day my mom explained to me that she put a lot of effort into preparing our lunch, and when I ignored her request to come eat she felt disrespected. She also told me that my actions did not make her feel appreciated because she chose to make a dish which required a lot of work.

After reflecting on what my mom told me, I realized that if I would have paused the game and came downstairs to eat lunch, two things would have happened differently.

First, I wouldn't have lost the opportunity to win the game because we could have been able to save our place and return after we ate. Second, and most importantly, my mother would have felt respected by the fact that we heard her, and that I urgently came downstairs to show gratitude for the fact she cooked us lunch. This is an example of how being respectful can make you and your parents get what you both want.

Jonah x 2

It was pickup time after a long, fun day at summer camp, and we were sitting with our groups in the gym. A few other people and I were playing Uno and everyone had three cards left. I was getting ready to lay down a blue "Draw Two" card for the player to my right when I heard my name called over the walkie-talkie.

I dropped my cards and hopped up to grab my bag at the same time as someone from another group did. We both looked at each other, confused. It turned out we both have the same name! I walked over to my counselor and asked him which Jonah they were calling for. They said the other guy, so he went downstairs to leave. So I went back to my group and sat down. Then out of nowhere the other Jonah abruptly came back and told me it's actually me. I got my bag and started walking to the door, and that's when I remembered my dad telling me this morning, when he dropped me off, we would have to rush to get my siblings before their daycare closed.

I started running as fast as I could to the door and down the stairs, so my dad didn't think I was being slow, or wasteful of his time. When I got in the car my dad immediately asked why I took so long. "I told you this morning when I came," he said, "that we were going to have to pick up your siblings before their daycare closed."
I told him there was confusion in the gym between me and the other Jonah, and when I found out it was me I came as fast as I could, because I knew we still had to get my sister and brother. I didn't want to seem like I didn't care about his time and what he has to do.

My dad then apologized and told me he didn't realize there was another Jonah, then said, "Thank you for rushing when you found out it was me, because that shows respect for me and what I have to do."

It's a Piece of Cake

On Sundays I stay home and watch my siblings while my dad goes to the store. He goes out to pick up groceries and other home essentials for the upcoming week, like food, paper towels and soap. One weekend, as I was showing my brother a game on his iPad, my dad snuck in the front door to let me know he was home with the groceries. My brother and sister jumped off the couch and ran over to him, screaming his name. I waltzed over to the front door and told him I'd help with the groceries. I ran to the car and grabbed as many bags as I could carry in each arm, and hurried inside with them. I started sorting the items he had bought so I could put them away more efficiently, while my dad started making dinner. As I was putting things away in the fridge, I noticed a bright red velvet cake in one of the bags. I couldn't wait to get a piece of that later.

When I finished putting the groceries away my dad thanked me for my help. I noticed that he was going to be making a big meal, and I knew it would take a while, so I took this as an opportunity to ask if I could ride my bike over to my friend's house. I had a feeling that the chances of him saying yes would be higher because I helped with the groceries and watched my siblings while he was gone. I told him I wouldn't be gone long and that I'd be home by the time dinner was ready—I definitely didn't want to miss out on a slice of red velvet cake for dessert! My dad nodded in agreement and told me to be home by six o'clock. I thanked him and ran to the garage to grab my bike, thinking about that velvety cake the whole ride over to my friend's house.

By helping with little things around the house, like sorting groceries and putting them in their respective places around the kitchen, it showed my dad appreciation for him getting the family what we need. Also, by going out of my way to do these things it showed him I'm respectful, which is exactly how I want to be viewed by my parents.

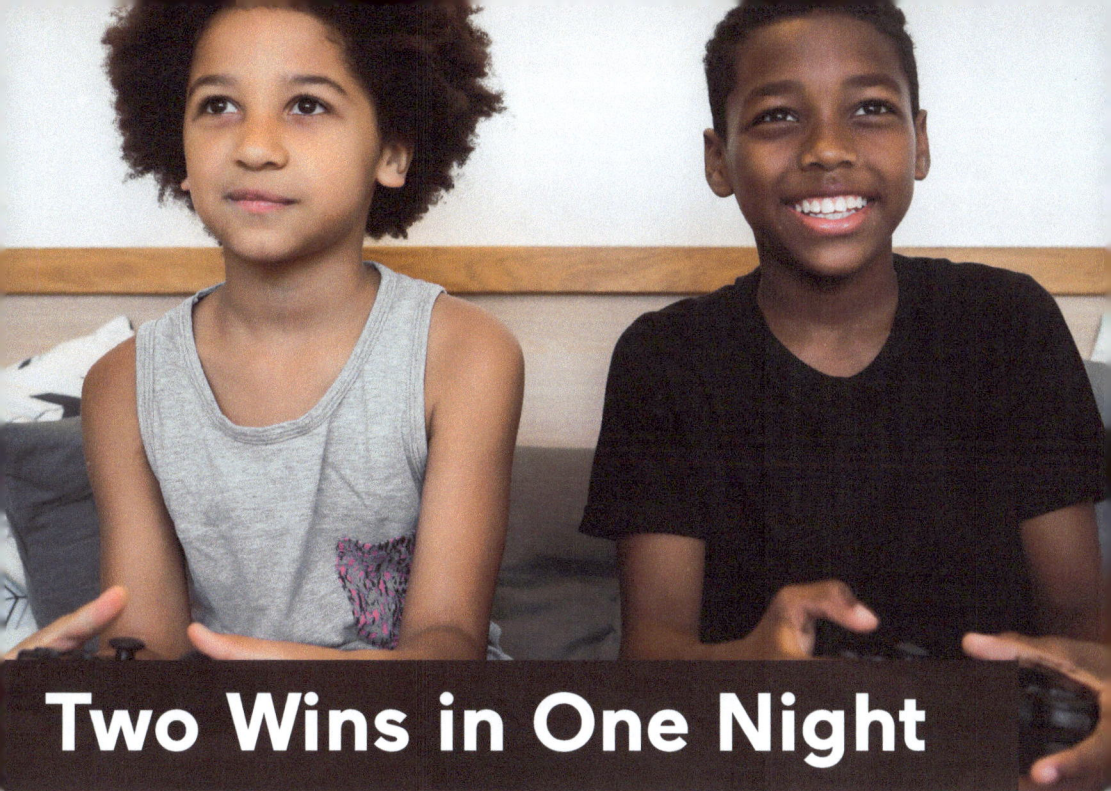

Two Wins in One Night

Normally on weekends I can stay up late, but on weekdays I have to go to sleep earlier so I'm well rested for school. On a typical school night, I take a shower before dinner. After dinner is when I usually watch videos on the internet, play video games, or call my friends, before getting ready for bed around 10pm.

I'm pretty good about time management and getting myself to bed before it's too late, but there are some nights when I lose track and need a reminder. One Wednesday night I was playing online on my PlayStation with some friends. It was getting kind of late when my dad peeked into my room and told me I could play for twenty more minutes before I had to get ready for bed. I was reluctant to do so because I was in the middle of a match. If you know anything about Fortnite, then you know it's not easy to win, so you have to take advantage of the times when you have a chance.

I didn't want to upset my parents, or risk staying up too late and not waking up in time for school in the morning, so I set a timer for twenty minutes to make sure I didn't forget. I went on to win the match right as the timer started going off. I said bye to my friends, turned my TV off, and texted my parents to let them know I had followed their directions; then I went to sleep.

Had I not acknowledged my dad when he stopped by my room to remind me of curfew, I probably would have stayed up all night with my "winner's high." My parents appreciate that I respect their time limits and curfews, which allows me to have more privileges—like more time on my PlayStation or my phone. And who doesn't want that?!

Thank You

Christmas has always been my favorite holiday. I remember when I was a little kid, around four or five, on Christmas that year I had gotten everything I wanted, but at the end of unwrapping all of my presents I didn't say "thank you." So my parents asked me, "What do you say?" There was a long pause, and I said, "I don't know." Without hesitation, they said, "You say 'thank you.'"

They explained that thanking others shows your appreciation for getting something you want, or for them doing something nice. It might also make them want to do something like that again in the future. To this day I still say thank you to people for most things I get. I might forget a little here and there, but I try my best to show people I appreciate the things they do for me.

Excuse Me

Interrupting what someone's saying or doing can come off as disrespectful. I learned this one Saturday when I was super bored and had nothing to do. I played video games, went outside, and tried watching YouTube videos, but nothing seemed to entertain me. I kept repeating this cycle, waiting for the day to come to an end, until I got a text message from a friend who lives down the street.

He invited me over to his house so we could hang out. We usually talk, play video games, have Nerf gun fights, and watch shows or movies. He also told me he got a new pool in his backyard that we could go in. So I found one of my old backpacks and packed a pair of swimming trunks and a towel, then I rushed downstairs to ask my mom if I could go.

As I was approaching her room I could hear her talking to my dad, but I went in anyway. I was halfway through asking her if I could go to my friend's house when they stopped me. My dad said, "If you see us talking, please wait until we're done, or say excuse me if it's urgent." He also told me it's disrespectful to interrupt a conversation, and that it can be perceived as selfish because you're basically saying you only care about what you have to say.

They told me to leave so they could finish their conversation. I came back a few minutes later when they were done talking. I was then able to ask if I could go to my friend's house. They both looked at each other, then said to be back before dark. I grabbed my bag, hopped on my bike, and rode over to his house.

From this story I learned that when you interrupt someone, you're being disrespectful and selfish, even though you probably don't mean to be. It's best to try and wait until a conversation has ended before you jump in, except for emergencies.

C'mon Bro

Parties are always fun to go to, especially when they are your friends or family. One Thursday I went to get the mail and noticed an invitation to my friend David's birthday party.

His party was on Saturday at four o'clock at a paintball center. I went back inside with the mail to show my parents the invitation. They both said I could go, then my mom texted his mom my RSVP. I played NBA 2K20 on my PlayStation online with him the night before the party, and he told me he had invited six other people so we'd be able to play in teams against each other. David and I stayed up playing NBA 2K20 for about two hours before saying bye and going to sleep.

The next morning I woke up and took a shower before getting ready for the party. It wasn't until I got in the car that I realized we hadn't gotten a birthday card. We knew we would probably be a little late to the party, but we couldn't show up without a card! We stopped by a convenience store and my dad ran inside to grab one. Once he got back, I signed the card and he put some cash inside before we started heading to the center. When we arrived, my parents and I went inside to meet up with my friends. I was the last person to arrive and they were waiting on me to start playing. My parents quickly said "hi" and "bye" to my friends, before heading out and leaving my friends and me to get ready for the first match.

We were directed to a wide black room on the side of the building to get our gear and learn the rules. After we put on our helmets, vests and elbow pads, we were given instructions and the rules of the game: no hitting or tackling, no throwing weapons, no shooting defenseless players, and play safe. While she was speaking,

I noticed one of David's other friends making noises and gestures, hinting that he didn't care about the rules. Then he interrupted the woman and asked rudely, "Can we go already?"

I looked at him and said, "Bro, just listen." He rolled his eyes and didn't say anything. I didn't even know this other guy, but I could tell he wasn't listening as she continued giving us instructions. At least he didn't say anything else.

After she finished, we got into teams, went outside, and got on separate sides of the field. Over a speaker we heard, "Three, two, one, GO!" My team was swift out of the gate and we won the first round. Luckily, I remained clean. Early into the second round I was pelted by a paintball under my left arm as I was running for safety behind a barrier. My side stung as I was walking over to the safe zone, so I took off my helmet to check it out. Out of nowhere, I felt the same sting on my leg as I had on my side. I looked down and saw yellow paint dripping down my leg. I had been hit again! But one of the rules was: no shooting defenseless players—so basically, don't shoot anyone walking to the safe zone or with their helmet off. I looked over to see where the yellow paint came from, and it was the same guy who didn't listen to the rules! Someone ran out and told him he was disqualified. He tried to explain himself, but he had already broken a different rule in the first round.

We went on to finish the next three rounds of our match before it was time to leave. When we got back inside, I didn't see the guy anywhere. I guess his parents got him and left. We spent the rest of the afternoon singing "Happy Birthday," eating cake, and playing games in the mini arcade before people started leaving. Once it was just me, David, and his parents left, we all got in their car and they drove me home.

If David's other friend had been patient, and listened to the rules and instructions instead of being rude and interrupting, he may not have been disqualified and would have been able to stay for cake and other games. From this experience, I learned that listening is a sign of respect, and respect is something that you need to show to everyone. Even if your parents aren't around for the moment, you still need to respect other adults, and even your peers.

When Did You Say That?

Have you ever been so focused on one thing that you tune out everything else around you? If you have, keep reading; if you haven't, still keep reading.

It was Saturday evening and I was playing Fortnite after coming back from the pool. I was in the middle of a match when I heard footsteps coming up the stairs. It was my mom. She came in and told me she was going to get her nails done, and said out loud a small list of chores that I needed to do while she was gone. I heard the first two chores, trash and laundry, but was too focused on the fight to hear the rest.

After she left, I finished the game then went down to take out the trash and transfer the clothes from the washing machine to the dryer. When I walked into the kitchen the smell of the trash hit me in the face. I covered my nose as I walked over to find my little sister's diaper staring right at me from the top of the trashcan. I tied the trash bag and took it out back and put it in the garbage can, then I went back to the kitchen and washed my hands before heading to the laundry room. Once there, I put all the wet clothes from the washing machine in the dryer and pressed "start," then I went back upstairs.

Once I got back to my room, I turned my TV back on and started watching Netflix. About an hour later I heard my mom's car pull in, and I went downstairs to greet her. She asked me if I completed all my chores. I told her that I did, then she started walking around the house to check. She made her way to the kitchen and looked into the sink. She asked, "Why didn't you put the dishes in the dishwasher?"

I paused, then said, "You didn't tell me to."

HOW TO GET WHAT YOU WANT AND MAKE YOUR PARENTS PROUD TOO

She looked at me sideways, then said, "Yes I did. If you were listening and not so focused on that game, you would've heard me!"

I apologized, but she instead pointed out that I forgot to clean the counters, too. She told me that I wouldn't be able to play on my PlayStation for the rest of the weekend because I didn't listen. I agreed that this was fair, and told her, "Yes, ma'am," then started working on the rest of the chores. Not listening to my mom was disrespectful and irresponsible. The consequence of my poor actions was me losing gaming privileges that weekend. Because of this, I learned to always put my parents' orders first. This shows great respect for them.

Mood Swings

I always get nervous when report cards are sent out.

One day after school, about two weeks before report cards were scheduled to come home, I found myself scrolling through Powerschool.com (a website that tracks our grades) to see how I had done that quarter. Everything looked good until I got to the bottom of the page and saw I had a low C in reading.

I thought about my C for a long time, then realized—school is a lot like football! Each quarter we get a report card which shows our scores, the same way a scoreboard would in a game. With fall semester coming to an end and winter break quickly approaching, it was as if we were getting ready for halftime. Unfortunately for me, it seemed as if I was on the losing team, because my missing assignments made for poor grades. Similarly to football, I also sometimes think of school like a job. I go there every weekday to learn as much information as I can to apply to assignments and tests. The best part of my job as a student is the pay. Bringing home good grades gives me the same feeling as winning a close football game. I know showing my parents a good test score or grade helps my chances of getting something I want from the mall or a store.

So I clicked on my grade to see what assignments I did poorly on or forgot to turn in. I had one homework packet missing and a worksheet missing, too. I immediately opened my backpack to check for those assignments, and saw both of them beside each other all done and ready to turn in.

I made sure to turn in the missing assignments for grading as soon as I got to class the next day. As soon as I returned to my seat, my teacher announced that our final assignment for the semester would be an essay based on the book we were reading in class. This would give me time to increase my score before "halftime" (a.k.a. winter break).

The essay would be a formal grade, so it could either boost my entire grade for the class up or bring it down. This was going to be very important, so I would have to study all my notes I wrote down in class. The day of the essay finally came and I had butterflies on the way upstairs to my classroom. I knew I was ready, but I was still nervous. When I began to write the essay, my nerves settled. I wrote the first sentence and then it was like thoughts started coming from all directions. I worked on writing all day and night before finishing it the next day in class. Once I finished I felt so relieved, like if I was carrying a thousand pounds on my back and the weight just fell off when I turned my essay in.

Grades were coming out the following week, so all I could do was wait. I was antsy with anticipation to find out my score. Monday arrived and I braced myself as I logged in to check my grades. I got a 93 on my essay, which brought my final grade up to a 92! I was so happy with my final grade, but all the stress leading up to the essay was rough. I made a promise to myself that next quarter I would pay better attention to my homework.

In this instance, I was responsible because I recognized my mistake of having a bad grade, and fixed it instead of brushing it off and waiting until next quarter. This can also apply to other aspects of life, like when I'm an adult and have a job, because if I make a big mistake it's my duty to fix it so I don't get fired. Even if I'm the boss I still have to fix my mistakes, because if my staff doesn't like something then they will not want to work there anymore.

Accountability

It was a rainy night and I had to roll the trash cans to the street. Every step I took, I could feel my shoes sinking in the ground more and more. I also was drenched in the first 15 seconds. I decided I would wait until morning when it wasn't so nasty outside. I made sure to tell my parents so they would know I wasn't slacking off on my chores. I also set my alarm a half-hour early so I had time.

When I woke up, I was exhausted but I wasn't going to lay back down, because I wanted to hold myself accountable. I put on a jacket and boots because I knew it would be cold and wet, rolling the trash cans around. When I got downstairs, I turned off the alarm and went outside. The grass looked soggy and everything was wet. I started rolling the cans around, my feet still planted in the ground; but I had boots on, so it wasn't as bad as when I had shoes on the night before.

When I got done I wiped my boots on the mat and left them outside, because I needed to come back to put the trash bags in the can. When I finished I put my boots in my room and went downstairs, where my dad told me good job for getting up and remembering to roll the trash cans in the limited time I had before getting ready. He also said I am very responsible, because instead of giving up on it I just waited the next day when the circumstances were better. This ensures trust between my parents and me.

Older Brother

Being an older brother can be difficult. From the lack of privacy to the constant distractions while trying to accomplish simple tasks, it's a chore in itself. Even though they can be distracting, I still like to help my parents out by sometimes watching my younger siblings. When I do watch them, I make sure to act as a role model for them. I enjoy doing activities with them—like teaching my brother how to read or my sister how to walk. Sometimes I do both at the same time!

For me it's important to teach and interact with my siblings so they know I care about them and want to see them do well. Another reason is because it helps my parents feel they can rely on me for other important jobs. I know I'm doing more than just helping my parents out. I'm being responsible because one day I might have my own kids I'll have to worry about. That's why it's so important to me to make sure I do the right thing, so I can be their role model and so they know the right thing to do.

When I help my parents it can sometimes be by getting my brother ready for daycare in the morning, or feeding my sister. By showing my parents how responsible I can be in my role as an older brother, it allows me more freedom and privileges, such as later curfews and more time to play PS4 with my friends; and I also increase my chances of getting something I want when I want it. A really big thing I do to help my siblings is teach them the importance of respect and kindness for others.

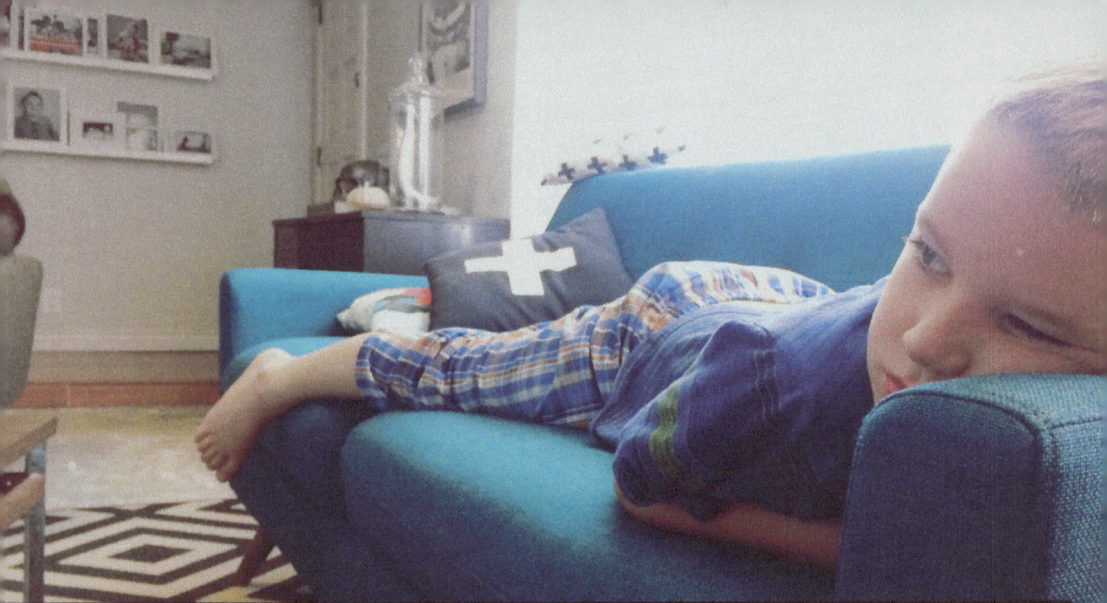

Bad Smell

Track practice is totally exhausting. I know I'm supposed to take a shower afterwards, but some nights I just want to be lazy. I got home from track practice one night and decided to plop down on the couch and kick my feet up.

No sooner had my feet hit the cushion than my dad came in and told me to get my sweaty socks off the couch. He reminded me that I always have to take a shower after practice or school, so I don't get the couch dirty or spread germs. I immediately went to take a shower to get all the germs and dirt off me. I got out and put on deodorant so I would stay fresh through tomorrow.

After drying off, I lathered shea lotion on my skin so it would stay moisturized. It's important to take care of my skin because it's an organ that protects the inside of my body. The last thing I did after getting dressed was brush my teeth. By doing so I was getting all the food that was caked on my teeth off, and I was keeping my teeth strong and clean. When I don't I can get cavities, and the extra food in my mouth can sink in my gums and cause bad breath, pain and gum infections.

By staying clean, moisturizing, and taking care of my oral hygiene, I'm keeping my body clean and the people around me will thank me.

Negative to Positive

Friday has always been my favorite day of the week. But just because it was Friday didn't mean I wouldn't have to treat it like a normal school day.

I was approaching the end of my day and my last class was Social Studies. Once I got in the class I saw that my teacher wasn't there. I noticed some people talking and joking around and I was tempted to join them, but then I realized it would be better if I just got ready for the day. We were supposed to be finishing a movie that day, so I was happy that we wouldn't have to do any work.

Once my teacher got there she told us that we wouldn't be able to watch the movie, because there was a test on Monday that had been assigned at the last minute. So instead we would be doing a whole class review with questions while she read. Most of the class started getting angry and having side conversations. I knew this test would be important for my grade, though, so I answered the questions and followed along in my book. I also knew I had to step up because most of the class still wasn't over the movie.

Once we got to the end of the lesson my teacher told us she was going to ask some review questions. The first question sounded familiar, so I looked at my notes and realized I had the answer written down. When I answered the question my teacher's face lit up, and I could tell she was filled with joy because I was paying attention.

At the end of class she pulled me aside and told me that I handled the movie incident well and did a great job answering the questions. She added that she would be sending a positive email home because I did so well. After that, I thought about how my parents would be happy because they would know I'm paying attention and being a leader.

Big Help

I remember a time when I realized how valuable my role as a big brother is to my family. It was the weekend of my parents' Bahamas trip.

My brother, sister and I were going to stay with my aunt and uncle, and we had to rush to get ready so my parents wouldn't miss their flight. The first thing I did was prepare my bags, then I got dressed and brushed my teeth. Once I was prepared, I went downstairs to help my parents get my siblings ready, when I realized no one was awake.

I ran as fast as I could to my parents' room to wake them up. When they got up, I told them I would get my brother ready while they got dressed. I raced down the hall to my brother's room and noticed that the worst thing had happened—he wet his bed. I knew there wouldn't be enough time to give him a bath, so I had to give him a quick wash-up. Luckily he was well-rested, so he didn't fuss while I got him ready.

After he was cleaned up and dressed, I saw my dad coming around the corner to get my sister ready. On a normal day I would go play some video games at that point, because I had helped enough already. But instead I put some waffles in the toaster for my brother and me, and put some applesauce in a cup for my sister, so my parents would have one less thing to worry about while they rushed to get ready.

By the time I was done preparing breakfast, everyone had their bags at the door and was ready to go. We headed to my aunt's house where my parents said their goodbyes, and thanked me for waking them up and getting the morning started. Once they left I told my aunt and uncle that Jade and Jalen had already eaten breakfast. Around one o'clock it was time for lunch and for Jade to be changed (her diaper was pretty stinky at that point), so I reminded my aunt. I continued in this manner the whole weekend my parents were away.

When they came to pick us up on Monday night, my aunt and uncle thanked me for helping them out all weekend and they told me that I was very responsible for looking out for my siblings. When my parents hear that I can look out for my siblings when they're away, they see that I am responsible.

One More Minute

I remember being woken up by my dad's footsteps one Monday morning before camp. He rushed into my room and ripped the covers off me while yelling, "Hurry up and get ready, we're running late!" I was really tired because I had stayed up all night talking to my friends and watching football repeats on ESPN. Instead of doing what I was told, I rolled back over for five more minutes of sleep. Shortly after I closed my eyes, I heard my dad yelling from downstairs, "Jonah, time to go!" I immediately jumped out of bed and threw on the closest pair of shorts I could find and a clean shirt. I sprinted downstairs, tripping over my shoelaces in my mad dash to the car.

When I got in the car and looked at my dad's face, I knew I was in trouble. I looked at the clock and noticed it was already after 10am. My dad had to drive me to camp before going across town for a meeting that was in twenty minutes! That was when my dad decided to have a talk with me about how I should have gotten up the first time he asked, instead of laying back down. When he was done lecturing me, I told him I was so tired because I had stayed up too late watching TV and talking to my friends.

We made an agreement that I would go to bed earlier on weeknights, especially if I would have to get up early the next morning. We also agreed that I would do as I was told from now on, and get up when asked—even if I was really tired. So I learned two things from this experience. First, I learned that I have to be responsible by going to bed on time. The other thing I learned was to follow directions when given. I like when my parents are happy, and following their directions is one of the best ways to make that happen.

Finish The Job

I can remember a time when I was watching TV in my room and went down for a snack. Once I got downstairs I noticed my clothes were in the dryer, so I took them out and put them on the table. My mom always folds them and puts them on the stairs for me to take up. After I put the clothes on the table I got my snack and went back upstairs.

30 minutes later my mom called me downstairs and told me that I was going to have to start folding my clothes too. When she said that, I begged to do anything but fold my clothes. I once tried it and didn't even make it halfway through. But my begging didn't work. My mom told me that because I was getting older, I was going to have to be more responsible by folding my own clothes and doing other chores for myself. So I started folding.

I had a random thought of what I would do if I was an adult and didn't want to fold my clothes. I would probably just have them laying everywhere, wrinkled and unorganized. So after I finished folding my clothes I thanked my mom for telling me to do it, because if she didn't my hatred for folding my clothes would just get worse, and when I go to college and have a dorm I wouldn't do it at all and would just have a mess. I told her that today I would start folding my clothes along with taking them out of the dryer, and she thanked me.

Lost Attention

It was just my parents and me until I was ten. I was always happy because it felt like I had all the attention in the world. I got new shoes once every two months; I was able to get toys from the store when I wanted; and I felt special. But that all changed the day my parents told me they were having a baby. When they told me I noticed my mother's face was glowing with excitement. I have to admit, I was kind of happy too!

As the initial shock and excitement of having a sibling began to wear off, I started to think about it more, and realized that a new baby would take most of the attention away from me. I got worried that I might not be as important anymore and that I would have to do everything by myself. I kept my thoughts to myself for a few days until I just couldn't take it anymore. I went to my parents and told them everything I was concerned about.

Once I finished they both told me that, yes, the baby will require more of their attention, but they will always love me the same and I will still be important to them no matter what. They also told me that this is a good thing because I'll learn how to be more independent and tend to myself.

Nine months later, the day finally came. No one knew at first because the baby came a few days early. My grandma picked me up early from school and her smile was bigger than usual. Once we got in the car she told me my mom had just given birth to the baby and we were heading there now. My heart instantly started beating faster than it ever has before, and I could feel sweat dripping down my forehead. I was officially a big brother! I didn't know how to feel. I had so many mixed emotions; I was happy, anxious, and kind of nervous.

Once we got in the hospital room I was flooded with emotions again. I was expecting the baby to be screaming, but he was quiet. My dad was holding him when I walked in but carefully passed him over to me. It was at that moment, just holding him, that I realized that I'm the big brother he's going to look up to. I have to show him right from wrong and help him learn.

Fast-forward to now. He's four years old and I've taught him more than I could have ever expected. Like how to wash his hands, how to say please and thank you, how to write and draw things, and more! To me, being a role model is important because there's only so much my parents can teach him, and if I already know what to do why not teach him?

You're Not Slick

I've always dreaded cleaning my room. I remember one time when I was told to clean my room, but I didn't want to because I was so into the video game I was playing. So I paused the game, put my dirty clothes under my bed, threw my shoes in my closet in a pile, and put little things like pencils and controllers in my drawers. Then I went to my doorway and scanned the room to see if it looked clean, and quickly un-paused the game and kept playing.

About an hour later my mom came to check if my room was clean. At first she looked around and it appeared clean. But right before she left, she turned around and noticed the clothes under the bed. Her facial expression immediately changed and she said, "What are those under the bed?" For a second I froze, then I just admitted they were my clothes. Once I said that I got ready for the storm of words that were going to come from her mouth.

But surprisingly that's not what happened. She simply said, "You need to have more self-discipline. I can tell you what to do but you still have to do it." She then added, "Eventually when you move out, you're going to have to tell YOURSELF to clean your room and then clean it."

I then said "yes ma'am" and cleaned my room the right way, but while I was cleaning I was thinking about what my mom said. It really opened my eyes to realizing that even with other things I have to do, when I grow up she's not going to be there to tell me to do it. So I might as well start doing things without her telling me to all the time, just to get used to it. It also shows my mom that I can do things without her telling me. When she knows this she can become confident in knowing I'll do something.

Slipped My Mind

Have you ever not wanted to do homework? Instead, you just put it away for later and have to do it at the last minute? Well, that is exactly what once happened to me. I had a graphing project for math class that my teacher gave us a week to do. I completed three of the four graphs on Tuesday and decided I'd wait a few days to do the last one. So Wednesday went by, and I didn't even think about it. Then a second day went by and it crossed my mind. At this point it was Thursday and the assignment was due on Friday. So I thought to myself, I'll just do it early in the morning before school, and I went to sleep.

But the next morning started with my dad waking me up because I slept through my alarm. That's when I got nervous because I knew I wouldn't have time to finish the project before I left. I rushed to get ready and planned on finishing it at school before class started. But there was one more challenge I would have to face: my teacher didn't let people finish assignments before class.

When I got to my class I immediately grabbed the assignment out of my bag along with a book. I pretended to read from the book and worked on finishing the last graph each time the teacher looked away. I kept checking to make sure she wasn't looking my way, and acted like I was reading when she did. I was doing well for a while, until I forgot to look up and she caught me working on my project.

Once she called me to her desk my stomach started feeling weird, and my heart felt like it was going to pound out of my chest. She reminded me of the rule, gave me a silent lunch and took off ten points from my final grade. I was so embarrassed about missing lunch time with my friends, and even more embarrassed when I got home and my parents asked me about the project. I was scared to tell them about losing points because I knew they would freak out and take away my PlayStation.

So from all of this I learned an important lesson—always finish the assignment while you're thinking about it. Now I make sure to hold myself accountable for assignments I need to finish, so I don't miss out on things like lunch with my friends or gaming after school.

Win Win Win

If you're competitive like me, winning can seem like the only option. Thinking about losing brings me back to a huge kickball tournament that I competed in at summer camp. There were eight teams who each had their own color. Two teams play at a time with the objective to be the first to reach five points. If your team loses, you're out; but if your team wins, you advance and get to play against the next winning team. The last two winning teams compete against each other to determine who will get extra pool time. When the counselor announced the stakes, everyone's faces lit up. It had been so hot out, I would have done just about anything for some extra time in the pool!

First up was the yellow team versus the red team. I was on the blue team, so I got to watch the two teams battle it out on the field, and look for their flaws. The yellow team quickly scored five points and the red team was eliminated. My team played against the green team right after and we absolutely destroyed them! Because my team won by the most points in the least amount of time, we automatically went to the championship round. Black and purple played a quick match and black won. Next up were the black and yellow teams, and the winner would play against us in the championship round. Both teams played a good game but the yellow team ended up winning by one point.

It was finally time to see which team would get extra pool time. The scoreboard went up fast when my team scored the first points right off the bat. Their first chance to kick didn't go so well. They struck out—once, twice, then three times—giving us the ball back. The blue team had a chance to win this! My team scored again. My confidence was at an all-time high and all I could think about was cooling off in the pool after this "W."

The yellow team was back at bat. Our pitcher rolled the ball towards the plate and it was like time was moving in slow motion. I knew before the ball even made it to the plate that this kicker was here to play. He kicked the ball super high, but not that far. My teammate ran under the ball to catch it but it slipped through his hands. The ball was still in play and the kicker was running. Instead of picking the ball up to tag the runner before he could reach a base, he put his hands on his head and started yelling at himself. The yellow team got their first homerun. After that, they had the momentum they needed and scored four straight points, beating us. I was so angry I didn't even shake the other team's hands. I knew I was supposed to, but I just didn't want to.

My counselor saw this and pulled me aside after the game. He told me that he was disappointed that I didn't show good sportsmanship after the game. I told him that I was 100% sure that my team was going to win, and I was so upset about being defeated that I couldn't bring myself to shake their hands. My counselor explained to me how important it is to act like a winner, even when you lose. It doesn't look good for you, or your team, if you act like a sore loser. And it won't change the fact that you lost, either. In the end, I learned that even if you lose the game, you're still somewhat of a winner if you display good sportsmanship.

Lack of Preparation

Have you ever worked really hard and put all of your energy into one specific goal? I did this once for a track meet. But not just any track meet; it was one that you had to be invited to. I was invited to the Junior Olympics, where the best of the best all around the country come to a small stadium to compete. Two weeks before the meet my dad got both an email and a letter in the mail saying I had been invited. When I got home from school he showed me the letter and I was totally excited! Later that night I started thinking about the meet, and it crossed my mind that my training would definitely get more intense; but I was confident that I was up for the challenge. I started training with my team four times a week instead of three. I also started to prepare myself mentally, and I improved my diet by decreasing my sugar intake.

After two weeks of focused training and healthy eating I felt ready for the race. The night before the meet, I packed some snacks and drinks to give me energy and keep me hydrated. Then I went to sleep. My dad woke me up at six o'clock so we could get there around nine or ten. Once I got my cooler full of things, I got in the car and went back to sleep. When I woke up, my dad and I were just arriving at the college where the stadium was. We parked, got our stuff, then made the long walk to find where my team was.

When we entered the stadium all I saw were people, thousands of them—from athletes to parents, coaches, and family members. Once we found my team, I put my stuff down and went over to my teammates while my dad talked to the coaches. They were playing card games and board games to make fun out of the wait. It would be hours until I would run my event. We joked and played until I heard the speaker say, "Eleven and twelve boys four hundred meter check in." That was my age group and the event I would be running. I and a few other guys who were running the same event went down to check in, along with one of my coaches. We got our lane numbers then went to warm up. Afterwards I went to sit down with the other seven people I would run against. I began to meditate to clear my head before the race, but I wasn't too nervous yet.

One of the helpers on the track walked up to the big tent and called my heat to come down. My nerves didn't start to kick in until I set foot on the track. My mind was only focused on the race and I felt adrenaline running through my body. I waited for five other heats to run and then it was my heat's turn. I walked to my lane when they called us on and went over my race strategy quickly in my head. That's when I felt an emptiness in my stomach and I realized I had barely drunk any water or Gatorade, and hadn't eaten any of the food I packed. At this point it was too late, and I could only pray that I wouldn't cramp.

That's when the person calling the race shouted out, "Runners, take your marks! Get set!" Pow! The gun went off and I ran as fast as I could, trying to hold that speed for the rest of the race. I was approaching two hundred meters which meant I was halfway done. I started to feel a minor cramp in my calves, but not enough to slow down. I was on pace to break my personal record of a minute and three seconds. But as I got to the last one hundred meters of the race, the cramp started to rise from my calves up my legs, and I could feel myself starting to slow down drastically.

When I got to the end I looked at the screen beside the track, and saw I had gotten a time of one minute and six seconds. I was devastated. I felt as if I let my team down, my dad down, but most importantly, myself down. I could barely walk back to where my team was and my coach had to come over and help me back. Once I got there my dad asked me what happened and I told him I cramped up at the end of the race. He then looked into my bag and saw I had barely touched any of the food in there. He didn't say anything else to me after that. He went to tell my coaches we would have to leave now because my mom was watching my two siblings alone at the house.

Once we were in the car and he got on the highway I told him I was sorry. He then said, "You should say that to yourself, because you didn't have enough self-discipline to make sure you were fresh and hydrated." He also said, "This should be a good lesson for putting your priorities first, instead of getting distracted and playing with your teammates the whole time."

So from all of this I learned that being disciplined enough to concentrate on the main goal you have going on is very important. It shows your parents that you can be independent and self-disciplined. You can still have fun with your friends, like playing games before a big race, but don't let that take away from focusing on your goals so you won't let yourself down.

Don't Hit Girls

If you have younger siblings like me, you know that you have to teach them just as much as your parents do. They won't know what's wrong unless you teach them what's right.

One day I went with my mom to pick up my brother and sister from their daycare. When we got there and went to their classrooms I noticed my brother was irritable. He was moping around, crying and tired. We got in the car and he went straight to sleep. I guess he was taking a power nap. Once we got to our house and I woke him up, I saw a totally different person. He was filled with joy.

We went in to eat our dinner. He went in the living room with my sister to go play while I made their plates. Out of nowhere I heard a smack! and my sister started crying. I ran over to see what was wrong, to find a guilty look on my brother's face, and an untouched toy between them.

I calmed my sister down and then I sat my brother on the couch. I asked him what happened and he said, "I was playing then Jade took my toy. I took it back then she hit me and I hit her back." I was stunned—he had never hit her before. I told him, "You can't hit girls! Especially your sister. You need to protect and care for her."

He understood what I was saying then went to apologize to her. I feel that as a big brother it's my responsibility to teach my brother and sister right from wrong, so they can take what they learn to self-discipline themselves when needed. By teaching my siblings the right thing, my parents see that I'm a role model.

Conclusion

You have come to the end of my book! I hope you enjoyed my stories and learned a few things that you can apply to your life. The main thing I wanted you to learn is there are lots of little things you can do to make your parents and peers proud. By being respectful, responsible, disciplined, and a leader, you can be the best version of you.

www.ingramcontent.com/pod-product-compliance
Lightning Source LLC
Chambersburg PA
CBHW041818040426
42452CB00001B/12